Rightly Responding to Jesus

HARRY BICKNELL

AN A–Z GUIDE TO DRAWING CLOSER TO CHRIST

Copyright ©2025 Harry Bicknell

All scripture quotations, unless otherwise indicated,
are taken from the Holy Bible, New International Version®, NIV®.
Copyright ©1973, 1978, 1984, 2011 by Biblica, Inc.™
Used by permission of Zondervan.
All rights reserved worldwide. www.zondervan.com
The "NIV" and "New International Version"
are trademarks registered in the United States
Patent and Trademark Office by Biblica, Inc.™

Cover Design by Kaisha Bicknell

Layout by Sandra Verhoeff

Typing of first draft by
Lana Thompson
Margaret Chambers

Editing by
Lori Bicknell
Dick & Sandy Brouwer
Jim Doan
Myrna Giesbrecht
Darrell Miller
Tom Powell
Steve Travers

Final Edit and Revisions by David Fields

*Without my editorial team this book
was a grammatical disaster and, quite
frankly, not worth reading. Thanks Team.*
— Harry Bicknell

Dedicated to my friends,
but more importantly
dedicated to those who are,
and will become,
friends of Jesus.

INTRODUCTION

Let me tell you how this book came to be written. In preparation for the 2010 Christmas Eve services at Summit Drive Church I began to search the New Testament to discover the ways in which people responded to Jesus Christ. It didn't take long to discover that people responded in both favourable ways: "Truly he is the Son of God!" and less favourable ways: "Crucify him!" One thing is for sure; Jesus elicited a wide variety of responses.

As I read and collated the varied responses to Jesus found in the New Testament, I began to ask myself the all-important question —How should we respond to Jesus today? I was not overly surprised to discover that the New Testament had much to say. Although surely not a complete list, I discovered 38 ways in which followers of Jesus Christ should respond to him.

To help me memorize at least 26 of these appropriate responses to Jesus, I developed a tool using the 26 letters of the English alphabet. This kind of memory tool is actually an ancient practice we see in the Bible itself. We see in Psalm 119 that each section begins with the corresponding letter in the Hebrew alphabet—a great way to help students memorize each segment of the Psalm. For the memory tool I developed the verbs I used are taken, in most cases, from the New International Version. In some cases I had to use another word (a synonym) to include all the letters of the alphabet. And, yes, when it came to the letter "X", I simply had to make up a word!

Personally I have found this memory tool very helpful. Once I had the 26 biblical responses memorized, I could review them at any time of the day. I often meditated and reviewed them as I fell asleep at night or as I was out for a walk, a drive and, as well, in times of trial and temptation. As a result, I found myself communing with Christ on a more frequent basis. It is my hope and prayer that you will memorize all 26 Biblical responses to

Jesus along with the corresponding verses of Scripture. If you do, I am sure you too will find yourself communing with Jesus in a more frequent, intimate, and meaningful way.

It is my conviction that discipleship to Jesus is the greatest privilege in the whole world. For this reason I encourage everyone to make responding rightly to Jesus the focus of his or her life. Although discipleship to Jesus is not simply about human effort (see Appendix I) we have a part to play, as the verbs found in the New Testament make so very clear. It is for this reason I titled this book, *Rightly Responding to Jesus*.

In His Love,

Harry Bicknell

PREFACE

This book is written based on the Apostle Paul's conviction that we were created *by* Jesus and *for* Jesus. As he wrote to the church at Colossae: "For in him all things were created: things in heaven and on earth, visible and invisible, whether thrones or powers or rulers or authorities; all things have been created through him and for him" (Colossians 1:16).[1] In my understanding, we exist because Jesus chose to create us. All that exists was his idea. By creation, we are his.

Furthermore, the verse says we were created "for him". In the words of Homer Kent, that means that Jesus: "...is the end for which all things exist and the goal to which all things must move." Therefore, it should be the goal of every follower of Jesus to learn and understand how we should appropriately respond to him today so we can truly honour and stay close to the One we were created by and for.

"The deepest desire of our hearts is for union with God.
God created us for union with himself:
This is the original purpose of our lives."[2]

— Brennan Manning

---

[1] The Holy Bible: New International Version (Grand Rapids, Michigan: Zondervan Publishing, 2011). All quotes are taken from the NIV.
[2] Brennan Manning, in *Wild at Heart* by John Eldredge (Nashville, Tennessee: Thomas Nelson, 2008) p. 119.

ALPHABETICAL TOOL

Rightly responding to Jesus, according to the New Testament, means we are to...

Ask for Things in His Name
You may ask me for anything in my name, and I will do it.
—John 14:14

Believe in Him
For God so loved the world that he gave his one and only Son, that whoever believes in him shall not perish but have eternal life.
—John 3:16

Call to Mind His Death
And he took bread, gave thanks and broke it, and gave it to them, saying, "This is my body given for you; do this in remembrance of me." —Luke 22:19

Depend On Him for Strength
I can do all this through him who gives me strength.
—Philippians 4:1

Enjoy Fellowship with Him
Here I am! I stand at the door and knock. If anyone hears my voice and opens the door, I will come in and eat with that person, and they with me. —Revelation 3:20

Follow Him
Then Jesus said to his disciples, "If anyone wants to be my disciple they must deny themselves and take up their cross and follow me." —Matthew 16:24

Glory in Him
Therefore I glory in Christ Jesus in my service to God. —Romans 15:17

ALPHABETICAL TOOL

Honour Him
...that all may honour the Son just as they honour the Father. Whoever does not honour the Son does not honour the Father, who sent him. —John 5:23

Imitate Him
Now that I, your Lord and Teacher, have washed your feet, you also should wash one another's feet. I have set you an example that you should do as I have done for you. —John 13:14-15

Join With Others in Following Him
And let us consider how we may spur one another on toward love and good deeds, not giving up meeting together, as some are in the habit of doing, but let us encourage one another—and all the more as you see the Day approaching. —Hebrews 10:24-25

Keep His Message Before Us
Let the message of Christ dwell among you richly as you teach and admonish one another with all wisdom through psalms, hymns, and songs from the Spirit, singing to God with gratitude in your hearts.
—Colossians 3:16

Look Forward to His Return
But our citizenship is in heaven. And we eagerly await a Saviour from there, the Lord Jesus Christ, who, by the power that enables him to bring everything under his control, will transform our lowly bodies so that they will be like his glorious body. —Philippians 3:20-21

ALPHABETICAL TOOL

Make Disciples for Him
Therefore go and make disciples of all nations, baptizing them in the name of the Father and of the Son and of the Holy Spirit, and teaching them to obey everything I have commanded you. And surely I am with you always, to the very end of the age.
—Matthew 28:19-20

Nurture Our Hearts with His Peace
*Let the peace of Christ rule in your hearts, since as members of one body you were called to peace. —*Colossians 3:15a

Obey Him
*If you love me, you will obey what I command. —*John 14:15

Please Him
*So we make it our goal to please him, whether we are at home in the body or away from it. —*2 Corinthians 5:9

Question Everything that Undermines Him
See to it that no one takes you captive through hollow and deceptive philosophy, which depends on human tradition and the elemental spiritual forces of this world rather than on Christ.
—Colossians 2:8

Remain in Him
*Remain in me, as I also remain in you. No branch can bear fruit by itself; it must remain in the vine. Neither can you bear fruit unless you remain in me. —*John 15:4

Serve Him
*Never be lacking in zeal, but keep your spiritual fervour, serving the Lord. —*Romans 12:11

ALPHABETICAL TOOL

Trust Him
Do not let your hearts be troubled. Trust in God; trust also in me.
—John 14:1

Understand Who He Is
But grow in the grace and knowledge of our Lord and Saviour Jesus Christ. —2 Peter 3:18a

Vocalize Our Allegiance to Him
Whoever acknowledges me before others, I will also acknowledge before my Father in heaven. —Matthew 10:32

Worship Him
And again, when God brings his firstborn into the world, he says, "Let all God's angels worship him." —Hebrews 1:6

Xtra Love for Him
If anyone comes to me and does not hate father and mother, wife and children, brothers and sisters—yes, even their own life—such a person cannot be my disciple. —Luke 14:26

Yield to His Leading
When they came to the border of Mysia, they tried to enter Bithynia, but the Spirit of Jesus would not allow them to. —Acts 16:7

Zoom In on Him
Let us fix our eyes on Jesus, the author and perfecter of our faith; who for the joy set before him endured the cross, scorning its shame, and sat down at the right hand of the throne of God.
—Hebrews 12:2

Ask for Things
IN HIS NAME

"You may ask me for anything in my name, and I will do it.."
John 14:14

My wife Lori and I had a difficult time conceiving children. Our first child came only after many years of trying, which included medical tests, drugs, charting, following "well intentioned advice" and, yes, prayer. Three years after the birth of our daughter, and with no second child, I suggested to my wife that we call for the elders of the church to come and pray for us. I really wanted another child and I so wanted a son.

In response, Lori suggested that we pray together at that very moment, and we did. The very next morning I received a call from a friend attending Regent College, on the campus of the University of British Columbia, asking me if I knew of anyone who was looking to adopt a child. My friend had heard through a professor that the daughter of an acquaintance of his was pregnant and had made the decision, along with the biological father, to give their child up for adoption. He said if I knew of any couple that was looking to adopt they should call Professor Michael Green to get the phone number of this young lady. In short order I did just that, and within a few hours I was talking to a young lady who would soon give birth to a child that my wife and I would officially adopt. And yes, the child was a boy! I will never forget this incredible answer to prayer. God gave Lori and I a very special gift.

Although I would readily admit that I do not get everything I ask for when I pray, that one incredible experience has encouraged me to keep asking for things in prayer. More importantly, however, Jesus himself invites me to ask for things in his name. As we read in John's gospel "You may ask me for anything in my name, and I will do it" (14:14).

Is Jesus serious? Is he speaking hyperbole—exaggeration for effect? Can we really ask for anything in his name and expect him to grant us our requests? The short answer is "yes". Yes, we can expect Jesus to grant us requests made in his name. Now let me give a more complete answer.

In John 14:14, Jesus is actually repeating what he said in verse 13: "And I will do whatever you ask for in my name, so that the Son may bring glory to the Father" (14:14). In addition, it must be noted that Jesus had just told his disciples that they were going to do even greater things than he did once he had left them and gone to the Father. Jesus was obviously convinced that his disciples would collectively be able to do greater things than he was able to do during his three years of public ministry. It is against this background that Jesus invites us to ask for things in his name, which would suggest that the primary focus of our requests should be about ministry issues pertaining to his rule in our lives.

Although I believe we can ask for things that do not directly relate to ministry and his purposes for this world, these things should be the primary focus of our prayers. That's why I am never surprised to hear that when people pray for opportunities to witness or to grow in their faith the answers are often "just around the corner". Our Father in heaven is obviously waiting for us to ask for the right things—things consistent with his will and purposes (cf. 1 John 5:14-15).

What things are you asking for in the name of Christ? I am convinced that we should all be asking for things in his name so that we can further his agenda and his purposes for our lives. I am also convinced that we should pray for things dear to our hearts. As we do, he will answer, giving us opportunities to give witness to the fact that our Father answers prayer when we ask in Christ's name. Never forget, Jesus is the one who invites us to ask for things in his name.

REFLECTION QUESTIONS:

1. What kind of things do you think God is most interested in giving us?
2. Why do you think it is important to ask for things in Christ's name?
3. What is one thing you should be praying about?

"I do not pray for success; I ask for faithfulness."[3]

— Mother Theresa

---

[3] Mother Teresa, <www.thinkexist.com>, accessed August 1, 2012.

IN HIM

"For God so loved the world that he gave his one and only Son, that whoever believes in him shall not perish but have eternal life."

John 3:16

Life is too short to allow us opportunity to do everything we may have dreamed of doing. We are limited in our time. As people often say, usually in their impatience: "I don't have forever!" The Bible describes our life as a shadow, a hand breath, and as a mist. Others verses use terms like vanishing, withering, fading and flying away to describe our fragile and brief existence. We, of course, know that to be true because we often say things like "oh, how time flies," or "where has time gone?" or "it just seems like yesterday."

In even more sobering terms, the Bible says we all have an appointment with death (Hebrews 9:27), and the statistics bear that out. Although the average Canadian lives 81.2 years, in many countries like Afghanistan, Botswana, and Mozambique the average life span is closer to 40 years. Truly, we do not have forever on this planet.

There is, however, good news for those who are looking for a solution to the brevity of life. The answer lies in the person of Jesus Christ. In John's gospel we read these verses: "Just as Moses lifted up the snake in the desert, so the Son of Man must be lifted up that everyone who believes in him may have eternal life" (John 3:14-15).

Let me briefly explain these verses before I discuss what is probably the most well-known and loved verse in all of Scripture. In these verses, we are reminded of an Old Testament story regarding a leader by the name of Moses. In the story, found in Numbers 21:4-9, Moses is leading more than two million people out of the land of Egypt and into the land God promised to Israel. Along the way, the people begin to complain against both God and Moses. They did not like the way God was providing for them. In response to their impatience, complaining attitudes, and lack of faith, God sends venomous snakes amongst them. In short order, the people see the error of their way and call out to God.

In response, God instructs Moses to craft a bronze snake on a pole with the instructions that anyone who is bitten by a snake could be healed simply by looking to the bronze snake. The solution worked. In a similar manner, Jesus tells us, men, women and children are saved by looking to Jesus—by trusting Jesus—who was also "lifted up" on a cross for our sins (John 3:15). The solution for our sin is to "look to Jesus," or as the most well known verse in Scripture puts it: "For God so loved the world that he gave his one and only Son, that whoever believes in him shall not perish but have eternal life" (John 3:16).

According to this verse, we can receive eternal life through faith in Jesus Christ. We do not have to work for it, earn it, or purchase it, for eternal life comes as a result of believing in—or trusting in—God's Son, Jesus Christ. The phrase "eternal life" is found 42 times in the Bible and the clear teaching of Scripture is that eternal life can be ours through faith in Jesus Christ.

Eternal life refers to both "life without end" as well as a certain "quality of life." Ultimately, eternal life is about living in the presence of God; free from tears, pain or death, in a sin-free environment marked by love, grace, and intimacy (Revelation 21:1-8). Although we can begin to "taste" what eternal life will be like now, we will never experience fully all that it means until we die or Christ returns for his people.

From the Bible's perspective, eternal life is the ultimate solution to both the brevity of life and the problem of death.

REFLECTION QUESTIONS:

1. Do you think most people are consciously aware of just how short life is? Would most people rather not think about it?

2. Why is it hard for some people to believe that faith in Christ is the solution to the brevity of life?

3. Why would it be important for you that eternal life is about both duration and quality of life?

"It is the rightful heritage of every believer,
even the newest in the family of faith,
to be absolutely certain that eternal life
is his [or her] present possession.
To look to self is to tremble.
To look to Calvary's finished work is triumph."[4]

— Larry McGill

---

4 Larry McGill in *The Christian Quote Book* (Grand Rapids, Michigan: Barbour Publishing, 2004) p. 81.

Call to Mind
HIS DEATH

"And he took bread, gave thanks and broke it, and gave it to them, saying, 'This is my body given for you; do this in remembrance of me.'"

Luke 22:19

For the last five or six years, a friend and I have gotten together to play a game of golf in memory of his brother; a man who was also a dear friend of mine. As we come to one particular hole, the one that was my dear friends' favourite, I find it difficult to hold back the tears; my memories of him are so rich. Many of us have such memories, don't we? We can think back on those people in our past who have profoundly touched us.

And most of us take time each year to attend services that help us remember things that are truly important. For example, we may attend a Remembrance Day Service to help us remember those who fought to give us the freedoms we enjoy today. On Thanksgiving Day, most of us attend a service focused on giving thanks to God for "every good gift" He has allowed us to enjoy. On Christmas Eve many will gather to celebrate the coming of Jesus Christ into our world—to celebrate the coming One who brings salvation and hope.

Whether it is practiced weekly or monthly, a key element of Christian worship is participating in a memorial act where we remember Christ's death for us. Jesus himself institutes this memorial meal—a meal of thanksgiving. As we see in Luke's gospel, Jesus instructs his followers to eat bread, symbolizing his body that is "given for you", and to do this in remembrance of him. "And he took bread, gave thanks and broke it, and gave it to them, saying, 'This is my body given for you; do this in remembrance of me'" (Luke 22:19). Throughout history, the church has taken Christ's instructions seriously and continues to remember his death through the celebration of the Lord's Supper.

In Paul's first letter to the Corinthians we discover some important information regarding this ordinance or practice that Jesus "ordained". In the course of rebuking the church in Corinth for the selfish manner in which they practised the Lord's Supper, Paul offers the church some key advice on the practise of remembering Jesus' death. In 1 Corinthians 11:23-26, Paul writes these timeless instructions:

> For I received from the Lord what I also passed on to you: The Lord Jesus, on the night he was betrayed, took bread, and when he had given thanks, he broke it and said, "This is my body, which is for you; do this in remembrance of me." In the same way, after supper he took the cup, saying, "This cup is the new covenant in my blood; do this, whenever you drink it, in remembrance of me." For whenever you eat this bread and drink this cup, you proclaim the Lord's death until he comes.

Based on this passage, we can make several observations:

1) Paul's teachings on the Lord's Supper were given to him by Jesus himself (23).
2) Jesus gave these instructions on the night he was betrayed (23). According to the Gospels, Jesus was celebrating the Passover meal with his disciples that evening. Note; the Passover was an annual Jewish celebration where the nation of Israel remembered God sparing their firstborn children and cattle because they had sprinkled lamb's blood on the sides and tops of the door-frames of their houses (See Exodus 11:1-12:30). Jesus now uses this meal of

remembering God's rescue of Israel from their slavery in Egypt to signify what he was now doing to rescue the whole world from sin through his own broken body and shed blood.

3) The practise of The Lord's Supper is clearly rooted in Christ's command to eat the bread and drink the cup in remembrance of him.
4) The Old Covenant (agreement) was established through the sprinkling of the blood of animals, whereas the New Covenant was established by the one-time sacrifice of Jesus, and the shedding of his own blood (Hebrews 9:14; 28).
5) Every time we participate in the Lord's Supper, we are proclaiming his death. We are telling ourselves and others of the great importance of his death.

I believe Jesus instructed us to participate in the Lord's Supper because he really wants us to grasp fully the significance of His death. Although the New Testament gives us over 50 reasons why Christ died for us, let's focus on six of these. Jesus died:

a) For our justification (Romans 3:24).
b) To demonstrate God's love for us (Romans 5:8).
c) To purify a people for himself (Titus 2:14).
d) So that we would live for him (2 Corinthians 5:15).
e) So that we would glorify him with our bodies (1 Corinthians 6:20).
f) So we could be forgiven (Ephesians 1:7).

It is no wonder Paul described Christ's death as a truth of "first importance" (I Corinthians 15:3)!

REFLECTION QUESTIONS:

1. How does participation in The Lord's Supper help you renew or strengthen your relationship with Christ?

2. Besides The Lord's Supper, what helps you reflect on the importance of Christ's death?

"We are told that Christ was killed for us, that His death washed out our sins, and that by dying He disabled death itself… That is Christianity. That is what has to be believed."[5]

— C.S. Lewis

---

[5] C.S. Lewis, *Mere Christianity* (New York, New York: Touchstone, 1986). First published in 1952 by McMillan Publishers, London, UK), p.56.

Depend on Him
FOR STRENGTH

"I can do all this through him who gives me strength."
Philippians 4:13

In the complicated yet intriguing movie The Tree of Life, viewers are invited to reflect on the reality and nature of human existence. After an unusual start to the movie, you are presented with the very tragic love-hate relationship of a young boys' with his father. His father was sometimes caring toward him but all too often he was harsh and even cruel.

Not only did this young boy have to struggle to relate to his unpredictable father, but he also had to struggle with his own behaviour. During a period of rebellion, he broke into a home, stealing a personal item, broke windows in a neighbourhood building, and shot his brother in the hand with his B.B. gun. As he reflected on his own disturbing behaviour, he came to realize that he did not have the power within to say "no" to harmful desires.

As I reflected on this movie and this young man's struggles with his own sinful nature, I couldn't help but think of the Apostle Paul's struggle with sin as discussed in Romans chapter seven, and my own struggle. It is against this everyday, universal struggle that the "empowerment" of Christ in us can be so encouraging. Paul knew very well that to live a life of contentment, joy, maturity and relative success in his struggle to do the right thing—including saying "no" to sin—he would need God's help. His words are still encouraging, still applicable, to us: "I can do all this through him who gives me strength" (Philippians 4:13).

Although the word "Christ" is not found in the Greek text, all scholars agree that "him" in this verse refers to Jesus Christ. So what does Paul mean when he says he can do "all this"—or as some versions translate "all things" or "everything"—through Christ who gives him strength? First of all, Paul is not saying that he can become anything he wants to be, or accomplish anything he wants to accomplish. Rather, Paul is saying that he can handle anything that comes his way as he seeks to promote the gospel.

Although Paul faced many difficult situations as he sought to promote the gospel (see 2 Cor 11:23-27), he could honestly say that he had learned "the secret of being content in any or every situation" (Philippians 4:12). So one must ask, what was his secret that enabled him to handle any and every situation? The secret is Jesus Christ. As scholar Ralph Martin said: "Paul was a man who had boundless confidence in the ability of Christ to match every situation he faced." Jesus works to give us strength in every situation we may face, and like Paul, we too can trust him. This is taught in many of the New Testament passages. For example, in Paul's letter to Timothy we read: "I thank Christ Jesus our Lord, who has given me strength" (1 Timothy 1:12; see also 2 Tim 4:7, 2 Cor 12:9). Jesus truly wants to help us. He wants us to come to him in times of need (Heb 2:16, 18 and 4:14-16).

What is it that you need strength for? Do you need strength to say no to temptation? Do you need his strength to help you deal with a very difficult situation? Do you need strength to forgive? Do you need strength to share your faith boldly? I am convinced that Jesus wants us to depend on his strength to face anything that may come our way. Furthermore, I believe he wants us to join with Paul in saying: "I can do all this through him [Christ] who gives me strength."

REFLECTION QUESTIONS:

1. What would keep you from seeking Christ for help?
2. In what circumstances do you think people most need Christ's strength?

"Jesus knows our every weakness, Take it to the Lord in prayer…
In His arms He'll take and shield thee, Take it to the Lord in prayer."[6]

— Joseph M. Scriven

---

[6] Joseph M. Scriven, lyrics to "What A Friend We Have In Jesus"

Enjoy Fellowship
WITH HIM

*"Here I am! I stand at the door and knock.
If anyone hears my voice and opens the door,
I will come in and eat with that person, and they with me."*

Revelation 3:30

One of my greatest joys in life is spending time with my adult children. To have a discussion over a meal, to watch a TV show or movie, or to simply "hang out" with them is something I really enjoy. In the spring of 2011, my daughter and I spent a lot of time watching the Vancouver Canucks' run to the Stanley Cup. More recently, my son and I spent a whole day playing golf together. I consider these moments as time very well spent. I am sure most parents would agree that having a positive relationship with their children is one of life's greatest blessings. Don't all parents long for a healthy, genuine relationship with their children?

In like manner, Jesus longs for fellowship with those he created. Even when we mess up, even when we are unfaithful in our commitments to him, he invites us to come back to him—to be in close connection with him. We see this clearly in the book of Revelation, where Jesus says: "Here I am! I stand at the door and knock. If anyone hears my voice and opens the door, I will come in and eat with him, and he with me" (Revelation 3:20).

This verse was first written to a church in the city of Laodicea (see Rev 3:14-22). The church of Laodicea was wealthy but tragically they had become complacent, self-satisfied, indifferent, useless in their mission for Christ, and sadly, ignorant of their true spiritual condition. Yet despite this condition, Christ invited these people to come back to him for fellowship.

In verse 20 Christ is portrayed as waiting outside "the door" of a person's life. Furthermore, he is not only standing outside the door of a person's life, but he is standing there knocking and hoping that disloyal, indifferent, and preoccupied people will respond to his invitation for fellowship. I say "fellowship" because the phrase, "eat with me", is symbolic of fellowship—of intimate connection and close relationship. In the first century, eating was the occasion for loving, intimate fellowship with friends and family. Jesus longs for fellowship with us whether we are faithful disciples, prodigals, or people who have yet to begin a relationship with him. It's amazing, isn't it? That the Creator of the universe longs to have fellowship with us? May we all continue to open the "doors of our hearts" to his invitation for genuine, intimate fellowship.

REFLECTION QUESTIONS:

1. Who do you really enjoy spending time with? Why?

2. What causes you to seek fellowship with Jesus?

3. What are some ways you can have fellowship with Jesus?

"A car is made to run on gasoline, and it would not run properly on anything else. Now God designed the human machine to run on himself. He himself is the fuel our spirits were designed to burn, or the food our spirits were designed to feed on. There is no other."[7]

— C. S. Lewis

---

[7] C.S. Lewis *Mere Christianity* p.54.

Follow
HIM

> "Then Jesus said to his disciples, 'If anyone wants to be my disciple they must deny themselves and take up their cross and follow me.'"
>
> Matthew 16:24

While attending a pastors' conference, I heard a most unusual story. Guest speaker Peter Unrau told the other pastors that he began each morning by stretching out his arms over his head as he said, "I surrender Lord—Yes I surrender to your leadership." That story has stayed with me for a long time, not only because Pastor Unrau was an engaging, funny and godly man, but also because surrender to Christ's leadership is one of the necessary responses Jesus requires. As we read in Matthew's gospel: "…If anyone would come after me, he must deny himself and take up his cross and follow me" (Matthew 16:24).

In this verse, Jesus is once again calling people to follow him. "Following Jesus," in the words of Joseph Stowell, "…is the beginning and end of what it means to be a Christian. Everything in between is measured by it." To be a Christian, then, requires that we follow Jesus in complete abandon to him and his ways. Together with other believers, we follow Jesus' teachings, his example and his Spirit.

This verse tells us that there are several things we must do if we are going to follow Jesus. First, we must deny ourselves. To deny ourselves is to say "no" to our sinful ego that seeks to put "self-first" so that we can truly be God-centred.

Second, and certainly related to the idea of denying ourselves, we must "take up our cross". In the first century, a person sentenced to death literally had to carry his cross to the place of his execution. So what is Jesus asking us to do when he says we are to "take up our cross"? In the Quest Study Bible, we find this explanation: Jesus is asking us "to commit our lives wholeheartedly to him, accepting any hardship this choice may bring." Tragically, for many people following Jesus has cost them their lives. In fact, more people lost their lives in the 20th century because of their loyalty to Jesus than in all previous centuries combined.

Third, the demands of following Jesus are very challenging, but they are not that costly in light of what Jesus goes on to say in the following verse. According to Jesus, it is only through surrender to Him that we find the life God created us for—only in surrender of our "self" do we find our "real life." As C.S. Lewis once said, "The more we let God take us over, the more truly ourselves we become—because he made us…It is when I turn to Christ, when I give up myself to his personality, that I first begin to have a real personality of my own."

Furthermore, nothing we could possibly gain in this world could compare to what Christ has for us in the life to come. He is coming back to reward us. To deny ourselves and to take up our cross is truly in our best interest, both now and forever more.

REFLECTION QUESTIONS:

1. How do you think a non-Christian would initially respond to the demands of following Jesus?

2. How would a proper understanding of Jesus make the demands of following him more acceptable?

3. In your own words, describe what it means to follow Jesus (You can write in the following space).

"The greatness of a man's power
is in the measure of his surrender."[8]

— William Booth

---

[8] William Booth, in *The Christian Quote Book*

Glory IN HIM

"Therefore I glory in Christ Jesus in my service to God."
Romans 15:17

Is it ever okay to boast of personal achievements? A wise man once said; "Let another praise you and not your own mouth; someone else, and not your own lips" (Proverbs 27:2). I believe most of us would agree with his advice, for no one really enjoys a braggart.

So let me ask a less obvious question: Is it ever okay to enjoy, delight in, or rejoice in a personal accomplishment? I think many of you would say, "Yes, it's okay," especially because the idea of "boasting" is no longer part of the question. Simply to sit back and enjoy, or even rejoice, in an accomplishment that came about by hard work and much sacrifice is something even the Apostle Paul would do. Look at what he says in his letter to the church of Galatia; "Each one should test his own actions. Then he can take pride in himself, without comparing himself to somebody else…" (Galatians 6:4). Frankly, I think there is great joy in doing the things God has uniquely called you to do.

Having said that, I think the apostle Paul—who we might consider one of the most intelligent, hardworking, interesting and effective human beings who ever lived—would be the last person to boast (see Gal 6:14). In his letter to the church in Rome he writes;

"Therefore I glory in Christ Jesus in my service to God" (Romans 15:17). What is Paul saying when he writes, "I glory in Christ Jesus in my service to God"? This may be the most difficult to understand of all the biblical responses to Jesus. However, when we read the whole passage in which this response is found, it becomes quite clear that Paul is simply rejoicing and delighting in the person of Jesus Christ. When Paul says, "I glory in Christ Jesus," he is most definitely not boasting about himself, but rather he is boasting about what Jesus was able to accomplish through him (v.18). Furthermore, Paul fully realizes that the ministry God gave him was a gift of grace (v.15), and that the effectiveness of his preaching must be credited to the Holy Spirit (v.16). Therefore when Paul says, "I glory in Christ Jesus," in essence he is saying, "everything I have ever been able to accomplish, or will accomplish, comes from Jesus."

Although from a human perspective one might say that Paul has reason to boast because of his sacrificial lifestyle, hard work, and far-reaching effective ministry, he would have no part in such boasting (See 2 Cor 11-12). For Paul, everything he was, everything he had, and everything he did was a result of God's unmerited favour—God's grace. If ever he was to boast, it would only be in Christ (Galatians 6:14), through whom he was saved and made spiritually alive.

Like Paul, we too need to learn to "Glory in Christ Jesus", for all that we have comes to us by grace. In the days, months, and years to come, may we "glory in Christ Jesus," for all that he has given us, and for all he will accomplish through us. As Paul wrote in his letter to the church in Corinth: "Let him who boasts' boast in the Lord" (1 Corinthians 1:31).

REFLECTION QUESTIONS:

1. What motivates a human being to boast in their achievements?

2. What would it look like for you to "glory in Christ Jesus"?

3. In the lyrics of a song by worship leader Martin Smith, he asks himself: "What would I have done if it wasn't for Jesus?" Take a few minutes to ask yourself that same question today. Take some time to "glory" in Jesus—in what he has done for you and how he has used you, even your weaknesses and failures, to bless others.

"Grace comes free of charge to people who do not deserve it and I am one of those people. I think back to who I was—resentful, wound tight with anger, a single hardened link in a long chain of un-grace learned from family and church. Now I am trying in my own small way to pipe the tune of grace. I do so because I know, more surely than I know anything, that any pang of healing or forgiveness or goodness I have ever felt comes solely from the grace of God."[9]

— Philip Yancey

---

[9] Philip Yancey, *What's So Amazing About Grace* (Grand Rapids, Michigan: Zondervan Publishing House, 1997) 42.

HIM

> "...that all may honour the Son just as they honour the Father. Whoever does not honour the Son does not honour the Father, who sent him."
>
> John 5:23b

During a recent eight-city tour in Northern European countries, I must have seen over a hundred statues erected in the honour of great men and women. These people were kings, queens, rulers, generals, admirals, poets, musicians, writers, politicians, and even a President of the United States of America. Some of these statues were quite modest, while others were magnificent works of architecture, such as the one in Trafalgar Square in honour of Lord Admiral Nelson. These monuments served to honour the leaders and heroes of these nations, recognizing their contributions.

Christians are also called to honour their kings or leaders (Romans 13:1-7), but more importantly, to honour Jesus himself. Jesus tells us in John's Gospel that God the Father entrusted him with the role of being the Saviour and Judge of the world, for the reason "...that all may honour the Son just as they honour the Father." And as Jesus goes on to tell us: "He who does not honour the Son does not honour the Father who sent him" (John 5:23b).

This is a serious statement. According to this verse it is absolutely crucial that we honour Jesus Christ because, if we do not, we do not honour the Father who sent him to earth. This verse obviously says something about the identity of Jesus, as a mere human would never ask people to honour him like they would honour God (See appendix IV).

The verses leading up to verse 24 give us several more reasons why Jesus is to be honoured. In verses 1-23 we see Jesus doing what the Father does—what only God can do. The Father heals, and so does Jesus. The Father raises the dead, and so does Jesus. Furthermore, since the coming of Jesus, the Father has assigned all judgment to him. For these reasons and more, we are to honour Jesus just as we honour the Father.

So we need to ask: "How can we honour Christ today?" I believe there are hundreds of ways to honour Christ today, like…

- Listening to his words and trusting him for new life
- Giving him glory when you are complimented for something you've done
- Letting people know that pleasing him is your top priority
- Committing to live in his ways—to listen to, and obey his teachings
- Giving him the right to direct your life

In conclusion, there are many ways to honour Jesus today. I don't think he is looking for us to build him a statue or monument but I am convinced he is looking for people who are willing to reflect his character and priorities by giving him their time, talents and resources to further his purposes. Ultimately we honour Jesus not with bricks or mortar but with a life lived for him.

REFLECTION QUESTIONS:

1. What does "honouring Jesus like we honour the Father" (John 5:23b) say about his identity?

2. What is the first thing that comes to your mind when you think of honouring Jesus?

3. What is the greatest way we could possibly honour Jesus?

"You are called Christian. Be careful of that name.
Let not our Lord Jesus Christ, the Son of God,
be blasphemed on your account."

— St. Cyril of Jerusalem (313-386)

Imitate HIM

> "Now that I, your Lord and Teacher have washed your feet, you also should wash one another's feet. I have set you an example that you should do as I have done for you."
>
> John 13:14-15

A friend recently told me the story of a 99-year-old man who was helping to teach young men about the Bible at a youth club. Even though the club would have upwards of 70 teenagers in attendance, this elderly man had the ability to keep their attention as he spoke to them about the love of God. This elderly man truly made ministry a way of life and I am sure he inspired my friend to do the same.

As I have watched my friend live out his faith, often in difficult circumstances, I have observed a person who thinks in terms of using his gifts, time, and resources to help others. Almost every time we meet, he will spend some time telling me about what he believes God is calling him to do. He has truly made ministry a way of life. Although inspired to serve by people like that 99-year-old man, and by his godly upbringing, my friend's ultimate motivation for service comes from Jesus Christ himself; the supreme example of humble service.

As we read the gospels it becomes very clear that Jesus is the ultimate servant. As we read in John 13:1-17, Jesus got up from an evening meal to wash his disciples' feet. Despite the fact that he was their "Lord and Teacher" (13:14), and God in the flesh (Jn

1:1,14), he was willing to perform the task reserved only for the lowliest of household servants. There is no other example in that ancient culture of a superior washing the feet of an inferior, but that's exactly what Jesus does here.

On the night Jesus washed his disciples' feet, he challenged the disciples with these words: "Now that I, your Lord and Teacher, have washed your feet, you also should wash one another's feet. I have set you an example that you should do as I have done for you" (John 13:14-15).

What a challenge! Jesus wants his disciples to follow his example of servant-hood. Said another way—Jesus wants us to imitate his pattern of humble service. In a world that so often is characterized by pride, self-centered living, and power seeking, Jesus calls his followers to imitate his life of humble service. Imagine for a moment: what a day it would be if every follower of Jesus Christ imitated his life of humble service. What a day it would be if every follower of Jesus—regardless of education, ability, position, wealth or power—patterned his or her life after Jesus' example. I have no doubt that a group of loving, humble servants who are truly dependant on God would have a profound impact in their homes, schools, work and places of recreation if they followed Jesus example. Let's join Jesus Christ in a life of humble service. According to Jesus, it's the way to a truly blessed life.

REFLECTION QUESTIONS:

1. Why is the question, "What would Jesus do?" such a great question?

2. How can, or how do you serve others in the context of your everyday life?

3. Why is following the pattern Jesus set of humble service such a wise way to live?

"Imitating Christ means that believers must stand against the cultural tides of upward mobility, adopting a mindset that follows the same trajectory of Jesus himself; namely, obediently serving the interests of God by being poured out for the sake of others."[10]

— David Fields

---

10 David Fields, *The Logic of Knowledge in Philippians*
(A Thesis Submitted to the Faculty of McMaster Divinity College: Hamilton, Ontario, 2007) p. 79-80.

Join with Others in FOLLOWING HIM

> "And let us consider how we may spur one another on toward love and good deeds, not giving up meeting together, as some are in the habit of doing, but let us encourage one another—and all the more as you see the Day approaching."
>
> Hebrews 10:24-25

After watching my son play football for over five years, I have come to the most obvious conclusion regarding the game: football is truly a team sport. For example, a typical high school team will have 30 players. The team success is entirely dependent on every player doing his part. A significant tackle or block could mean the difference between winning and losing the game. So although a team will have its well-known stars, the weakest player might make the play that determines the outcome of the game. I once watched a player who didn't see much playing time block an extra point conversion that proved to be the key to his team's victory. Football is a team sport. You cannot play football by yourself. In the same way, following Jesus is not simply a personal relationship with him—the life of faith is something we must do with other believers.

The corporate nature of following Jesus is found throughout the New Testament, but never more clearly than in Paul's first letter to the church in Corinth. In chapter 12 of that letter we learn much about the corporate nature of following Jesus. For example, in this chapter we learn that...

- We all have spiritual gifts to help one another grow and flourish in life (12:7, 28-30)
- Together we form one body (12:12)
- We all share together in the Holy Spirit (12:13)
- We are dependent on one another (12:14-21)
- We must have equal concern for one another (12:25)

For these reasons, we should not even think of trying to follow Jesus as if it was simply a private activity. Christianity is deeply personal, but never private. We truly belong to one another (Romans 12:5), and following Jesus must be done in community with others. We should not be surprised then that the writer of the book of Hebrews challenges us with these words: "…let us not give up meeting together, as some are in the habit of doing, but let us encourage one another—and all the more as you see the Day approaching" (Hebrews 10:25). Gathering with other followers is both an opportunity to encourage, and be encouraged, in our walk with Jesus.

Although following Jesus most certainly has a personal dimension to it, one must never overlook the deeply corporate nature of it. May it always be said that we have joined with others in following Jesus.

REFLECTION QUESTIONS:

1. How does our culture discourage us from focusing on the corporate nature of following Jesus?

2. How has the Body of Christ—the Church—helped you to follow Jesus?

3. What "gifts" has the Spirit given you to help others follow Jesus?

"By becoming a Christian, I belong to God
and I belong to my brothers and sisters.
It is not that I belong to God and then
make a decision to join a local church.
My being in Christ means
being in Christ with those others
who are in Christ.
This is my identity.
This is our identity."[11]

— Tim Chester and Steve Timmis

---

[11] Tim Chester and Steve Timmis, *Total Church: A Radical Reshaping around Gospel and Community* (Wheaton, Illinois: Crossway Books, 2004) p. 41.

Keep His Message Before Us

" Let the message of Christ dwell among you richly
as you teach and admonish one another with all wisdom
through psalms, hymns, and songs from the Spirit,
singing to God with gratitude in your hearts."

Colossians 3:16

During the first few months of 2009, Summit Drive Church gave out 1,000 copies of the New Testament. About 500 of these New Testaments were given to those who attend our church with the challenge to read through it in 2009. The other 500 copies were given to friends and acquaintances for the purpose of sharing the good news about Jesus. Although we will never know the full impact of challenging the church to read through the entire New Testament, or the results of giving out 500 copies to friends and acquaintances, I would do it again in a heartbeat, because through Scripture we discover God's will for our lives and most importantly, through Scripture we are led into a saving relationship with Jesus Christ.

The apostle Paul understood deeply the importance of God's word in the lives of believers, and often exhorted believers to reflect on the message and implications of the gospel. For example, in his letter to the Colossian church, Paul wrote: "Let the message of Christ dwell among you richly as you teach and admonish one another with all wisdom through psalms, hymns, and songs from the Spirit, singing to God with gratitude in your hearts" (Colossians 3:16).

In this verse, the "message of Christ" refers to the gospel of Jesus Christ (the good news that through Jesus' death and resurrection we can be put in right-relationship with God) and to the teachings of Jesus. It was Paul's deep conviction that as we let the "message of Christ" become deeply rooted in our hearts and minds, we can then pass on to other believers the practical and far-reaching implications of both the gospel and the teachings of Jesus.

As believers, we need to continually remind ourselves that through the gospel we are forgiven and restored to fellowship with God; that we are now children of God, free from condemnation, indwelt by the Spirit and destined to become like Christ. The good news of the gospel is something we need to hear over and over again as we let its profound implications transform our entire beings. That's why I have often said: "Preach the gospel to yourself, and do it often."

Likewise, the teachings of Christ—the very words of Jesus himself—need to be heard over and over again. Who doesn't need to be reminded of the importance of loving people, of forgiving those who offend us, of serving others, of praying for all, including our enemies, and of seeking first the Kingdom of God? We all do. We all need to be reminded of the gospel and the teachings of Christ.

And it's by living in community with other believers that we are best reminded of these great truths. So may we all give ourselves to the reading and study of God's word so that we can "teach and admonish one another with all wisdom." Yes, let's keep the "message of Christ" before us so that together we will encourage both ourselves, and those who are part of our church family.

REFLECTION QUESTIONS:

1. "One must always have a plan to feed one's soul or it simply will not happen." Agree? If so why?
2. How do you feed yourself spiritually? (See Appendix II)
3. Does Colossians 3:16 imply that all believers should, in some ways, be "teachers" of the gospel?

"Most of us do not need to learn anything new, but rather we need to be reminded of what we have already been taught."

— Samuel Johnson

Look Forward to HIS RETURN

> "But our citizenship is in heaven. And we eagerly await a Saviour from there, the Lord Jesus Christ, who, by the power that enables Him to bring everything under his control, will transform our lowly bodies, so that they will be like his glorious body."
>
> Philippians 3:20-21

Our physical bodies will eventually wear out. As I sit here writing this chapter, I am aware of friends who have…

- Heart related problems
- On-going joint and back pain
- Wrist and hand problems
- Hip problems
- Trouble remembering what they said five minutes ago
- Legs that no longer function
- Increasingly diminished sight, hearing and flexibility
- Cancerous growths
- Chemical imbalances

Maybe you can relate? Or maybe you know and love people whose bodies are failing? The reality is that our bodies will eventually wear out. Even if we eat well, exercise often, and have a very positive outlook, our physical bodies are subject to the aging process. We cannot and should not deny the aging process, but neither should we deny or ignore what is promised to us as followers of Jesus Christ.

In Paul's letter to the church in Philippi we read these comforting, hopeful, words: "But our citizenship is in heaven. And we eagerly await a Saviour from there, the Lord Jesus Christ, who by the power that enables him to bring everything under his control, will transform our lowly bodies, so that they will be like his glorious body" (Philippians 3:20-21).

The Apostle Paul wrote these verses to help us stand firm in the Lord. Verse 20 begins by reminding us that ultimately we are citizens of heaven, and that as citizens of heaven we are to live by its values rather than the values of this world. Secondly, as citizens of heaven, we are to "eagerly" look forward to the second coming of Jesus. Wouldn't an eager expectation of his return help protect us from giving into earthly temptations? I believe so.

According to verse 21, Christ has the power to bring everything under his control and he plans to use that power to transform our lowly bodies to be like his glorious body. Although our present bodies are fearfully and wonderfully made, they are still lowly, meaning they are subject to disease, sin, aging and ultimately death. Christ, however, has promised to transform our bodies so that they will be made fit for eternity with him. This is what followers of Christ are to believe—and look forward to! To do so will not only help us to stand firm in the Lord but as well, it will help us to face difficulties of many kinds, including the aging process. For followers of Jesus, the best is always yet to come.

REFLECTION QUESTIONS:

1. How can "health concerns" strengthen our faith?

2. What does it mean for you to eagerly await Christ's return?

3. How does it affect you to know that your body will one day be like Christ's glorious body?

"This earthly body is slow and heavy in all its motions,
listless and soon tired with action.
But our heavenly bodies shall be as fire;
as active and nimble as our thoughts are."[12]

— Benjamin Calamy

---

[12] Benjamin Calamy in *Heaven* by Randy Alcorn (Grand Rapids, Michigan: Tyndale Publishing, 2004) p. 293.

Make Disciples
FOR HIM

> "Therefore go and make disciples of all nations, baptizing them in the name of the Father and of the Son and of the Holy Spirit, and teaching them to obey everything I have commanded you. And surely I am with you always, to the very end of the age."
>
> Matthew 28:19-20

In the spring of 2011, Summit Drive Church was in the process of hiring another pastor to work exclusively with teenagers. We had applicants from at least five different provinces and from two different states. The applicants were either just out of Bible College or had been in ministry for quite some time. In my opinion, many of the applicants were well qualified and could have done a good job ministering to the young people at our church.

In the process of interviewing and reading the more than sixteen plus resumes I came across a comment that grabbed my attention. One of the candidates said, "Whatever I do with youth I try to bring them one step closer to Jesus." When I questioned him about what he meant by that he said, "Whether I am teaching, leading worship or simply 'hanging out' with youth, I am always seeking to move them into a closer relationship with Jesus."

In essence, that is what making disciples is all about. As a church, we are in the business of helping people become faithful followers of Jesus Christ. As Jesus commanded his first followers, and us today: "Therefore, go and make disciples of all nations, baptizing them in the name of the Father and of the Son and of the Holy Spirit and teaching them to obey everything I have commanded you. And surely I am with you to the very end of the age" (Matthew 28:19-20). These verses in scripture are part of a larger passage that has been entitled "The Great Commission" in many English editions of the Bible. In many ways it is a great title for the passage because Jesus is asking his followers to engage in a worldwide ministry. Jesus is looking to have faithful followers in every country of this world. Friends, Jesus has given us a big assignment.

These verses teach us that the discipleship process should be characterized by two very important activities. Firstly, as we make disciples, we need to baptize them in the name (singular) of the Father and of the Son and of the Holy Spirit (many scholars see this baptism formula as evidence of the Trinity). Secondly, we need both to teach what Jesus taught and to model his ways in our own actions so others can enter into a life of genuine discipleship.

The Great Commission, as given by Jesus, demands a great response. Let me say it again, the Great Commission demands a great response. As a local church, we must see to it that we make discipleship to Jesus our top priority. In every possible way, we need to encourage people to begin a relationship with Jesus. Then, once that relationship has begun, we need to encourage them to be baptized as they declare their allegiance to him. In addition we need to make obedience to the teachings of Jesus the "front and center" of all we do as a church.

Over ten years ago Summit Drive Church developed a mission statement based on the Great Commission, which reads: "We exist to develop caring, passionate followers of Jesus Christ." (Please see the fuller statement in Appendix III). I am so grateful for this mission statement because it's rooted in Scripture and provides us with clear direction in all our thinking and planning.

And one last thing: In the last part of verse 20, Jesus promises to be with us as we seek to make disciples. The Great Commission demands a great response, but it also comes with a *great promise*. As we carry out his commission, Jesus promises: "I will be with you always, even to the end of the age." We can count on the *great promise* of Jesus' *great presence*, as we make a *great response* to the Great Commission.

REFLECTION QUESTIONS:

1. In your own words how "big" is the Great Commission?
2. What role do you play as your church seeks to make disciples?
3. How well do you feel you know, and can articulate, the teachings of Jesus? (Off the top of your head, how many commands of Jesus can you articulate? Maybe consider re-reading Matthew's gospel as a way of getting better acquainted with the commands and teaching of Jesus).

"Whatever I do with youth,
I try to bring them one step closer to Jesus."

— Jordan Pilgrim

Nurture Our Hearts with HIS PEACE

> "Let the peace of Christ rule in your hearts,
> since as members of one body you were called to peace."
> Colossians 3:15

Many things can bring us down, cause anxiety, upset us, or prompt us to worry. As I write this chapter, I realize there are many troubling events taking place in our world such as the riots in Vancouver, riots in England, volatile stock markets, wars in Afghanistan, Iraq, and Libya, the debt crisis in America, and the famine in Somalia. In addition to these major world events, we have to deal with every day common experiences like unexpected expenses, conflicts with people, unfair criticisms, health issues, loss of loved ones and other challenges that can often overwhelm us. All of these things threaten to rob us of our peace. I find Paul's words to the church in Colossae encouraging: "Let the peace of Christ rule in your hearts, since as members of one body you were called to peace" (Colossians 3:15).

The Jewish concept of peace *(shalom)*, which Paul certainly has in mind here, includes the idea of "wholeness" and "completeness" —it means that all our relationships are restored and as they should be. In the New Testament the word peace is applied to believers both in regards to their relationship with God and other people in an "outward" sense, and within each believer them self in an "inward" sense.

Now, by "outward" I mean that we can know we have peace with God through faith in Jesus Christ (Romans 5:1). Although at one time we were once enemies of God, we can now say that we have been reconciled to God through Jesus' death on the cross (Colossians 1:21-22). In addition to this wonderful fact, it should also be stated that Christ's death aimed at bringing people of all races into "one body" (Ephesians 2:15-16). Furthermore, all members of this "one body" are now to work toward harmonious relationships (Romans 14:19).

When we speak of the peace of God, or the peace of Christ, we must also speak of the subjective—or "inward"—aspect that Christ truly wants us to experience. As we read in Paul's letter to the church in Philippi: "Do not be anxious about anything, but in everything, by prayer and petition, with thanksgiving, present your requests to God. And the peace of God, which transcends all understanding, will guard your hearts and your minds in Christ Jesus" (Philippians 4:6-7). According to verse six, we can experience God's peace in our lives through the practise of prayer.

In Colossians 3:15 I believe Paul is referring to both the outward, objective aspect of peace and the inward, subjective aspect of peace. I say objective because the verse speaks of us being called to peace with each other—as members of one body. In addition, I think Paul is also speaking about the subjective, inward aspect of the peace of Christ when he exhorts us to let his peace "rule in our heart". To let "the peace of Christ rule" our hearts is to let his peace function as a guide so that we can stay calm, free from worry and anxiety, regardless of our circumstance. In their one volume Bible commentary, Bible teachers Walvoord and Zuck define peace as "God-given tranquility." We all need God-given tranquility to help face whatever happens in our all too often chaotic world, don't we? So let us nurture our hearts with the peace of Christ and may his peace truly rule over our inner lives. And let us never forget that Jesus is the Prince of Peace (Isaiah 9:6) who truly wants to give us His peace (John 14:27).

"Now may the Lord of peace himself give you peace at all times and in every way" (2 Thessalonians 3:16).

REFLECTION QUESTIONS:

1. What threatens to rob your heart of peace?
2. How might knowing you have peace with God affect how you respond to difficult circumstances in your life?
3. In what area of your life do you need to let Christ's peace rule your heart? Invite Jesus to give you his peace in that area.

"The secret of peace within and power without is to be always occupied with Christ."

— E. Schyler English

Obey HIM

"If you love me, you will obey what I command."

John 14:15

Several months ago a friend came to talk to me about something he felt God wanted him to do. As he shared with me I quickly realized that he was between "a rock and a hard place." If he did not obey God, he would not have peace, and if he did obey, he ran the risk of being misunderstood by the person he needed to talk to. In the end, he acted on what God had called him to do, and it turned out well. As I have reflected upon my friend's dilemma I couldn't help but think how delighted God must have been to observe one of his children seeking to obey him, despite the awkwardness and difficulty of his assignment.

In John's gospel, Jesus says much about the importance of obedience. For example, in John chapters 13 and 14 we find the following verses: "If you love me, you will obey what I command" (14:15). "Whoever has my commands and obeys them, he is the one who loves me" (14:21a). "Jesus replied, if anyone loves me, he will obey my teaching" (14:23a). "If you obey my commands, you will remain in my love, just as I have obeyed my Father's commands and remain in his love" (15:10). "You are my friends if you do what I command" (15:14).

According to Jesus, if you say you love him you will obey him. If you want to be considered his friend, you will keep his commands. So followers of Christ must ask themselves the all-important question: "What are his commands that I must seek to obey?" In the New Testament we discover many commands such as the commands to forgive, to avoid worry, and to serve others; but none greater than the command to love. Furthermore, it is very interesting to see the close proximity of the commands to obey Jesus and his command to love one another, in John chapter 15. For example, in John 15:10, Jesus challenges us to obey him, then in verse 12 he says: "My command is this: Love each other as I have loved you" (15:12). Likewise, following his command to obey him in verse 14, Jesus says: "This is my command: Love each other" (15:17).

It appears that the command Jesus is most concerned about is that we love one another. Not only does Jesus recognise that loving others is the second part of the greatest commandment (Matthew 22:39), he also wants love for others to be his disciples' distinguishing characteristic; as he says in John 13:35: "By this all men will know that you are my disciples, if you love one another." It should not surprise us, then, that the commands to obey Jesus and the commands to love others are so closely tied together in John's gospel.

Once again, consider with me the dilemma my friend was facing. If he really loved Jesus would he not obey him? And if he really loved his brother in Christ, would he not share what God had impressed on his heart, even if it was difficult to share? Obedience and love are always connected. We can't do one and not the other. As followers of Christ may it be said of us that we both obeyed Christ from our hearts and that we loved others with a sincere love.

REFLECTION QUESTIONS:

1. Why is obedience an appropriate response to Jesus?

2. How do you think Jesus responds to obedient disciples? (See John 14:27)

3. Which of Christ's commands is the most difficult for you to obey?

"Obey God in the things he shows you, and instantly the next thing is opened up. God will never reveal more truth about himself until you have obeyed what you know already…."[13]

— Oswald Chambers

---

[13] Oswald Chambers, *My Utmost For His Highest*
(Grand Rapids, Michigan: Barbour Publishing, 1997. Originally published in England, 1927).

Please HIM

> "So we make it our goal to please Him,
> whether at home in the body or away from it."
>
> 2 Corinthians 5:9

If you have ever have the great privilege of going on a cruise ship, you will soon discover that the staff "aims to please" the passengers. No request seems to be too small or too great. The staff will often memorize your names, greet you throughout the day, and say things like, "I hope you have a good day in Stockholm," or whatever city you are visiting that day. From my experience, the quality of service is second to none.

One might ask, "Why do the staff on a cruise aim to please the passengers? Is the staff looking to keep their jobs for a company that prides itself on service? Are they looking for promotions along with the wages that come with those promotions? Have some of the staff members found pleasing others to be an enjoyable way to live? Is serving others an integral part of their worldview?" Whatever their motivation the staff on cruise ships really do "aim to please" the passengers.

In a similar manner, followers of Christ should also have an "aim to please" approach to life. As Paul wrote in his second letter to the church in Corinth: "So we make it our goal to please him, whether at home in the body or away from it" (2 Corinthians 5:9).

In one short sentence Paul gives us his ultimate goal in life, or you might say, his philosophy of life. Why does Paul—along with his coworkers—believe "pleasing Jesus" is the key to life? The context of this verse shows us.

Firstly, Paul says he aims to please the Lord because we all have an appointment before "the judgement seat of Christ," where we give an account of how we have lived our lives (2 Cor 5:10). (Keep in mind this is not a judgement to determine our destiny, but rather a judgement "that everyone may receive what is due them for the things done while in the body, whether good or bad" v.10b). For this reason then, Paul wants to please Christ; knowing that he—and all of us—will be evaluated for how we lived.

Secondly, I believe Paul would say that he aims to please Christ because being with him is his heart's desire. Somehow, Paul had come to the place in his life where he could honestly say: "I would prefer to be away from the body and at home with the Lord" (2 Corinthians 5:8). When someone has that kind of passion to be with Christ, you can begin to understand why he or she would also say: "I make it my goal to please him."

Thirdly, I believe Paul made pleasing Christ his life's goal because he has personally experienced the love of Christ. He knew Christ loved him so much that he died for him (See Gal 2:20). If Christ loved him enough to give his life in Paul's place, how could he not live for him? "And he died for all, that those who live should no longer live for themselves but for Him who died for them and was raised again" (2 Corinthians 5:15). For Paul, no sacrifice was too great when it came to living for Jesus.

In conclusion, Jesus could say that he always did what pleased his Father (John 8:29). Although we will never be able to say we always please Christ, may we be able to say, like Paul, that: "We make it our goal to please Him".

REFLECTION QUESTIONS:

1. Who is it that most people today are ultimately seeking to please?

2. Carefully read 2 Corinthians 5 and answer the question: "Why did Paul make it his goal to please Jesus?"

3. What would help you to live out this Christian goal or philosophy of life where we are first and foremost seeking to please Jesus?

"When I came to see what Jesus Christ did for me, it didn't seem too hard to give up all for him. It seemed just common, ordinary honesty."[14]

— C.T. Studd

---

14 C.T. Studd in *The Christian Quote Book*

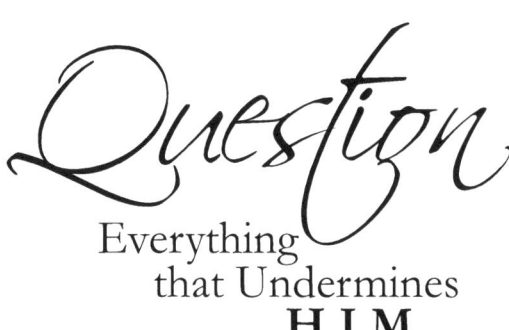

Question
Everything that Undermines
HIM

> "See to it that no one takes you captive through hollow
> and deceptive philosophy, which depends on human tradition
> and the elemental spiritual forces of this world rather than on Christ."
>
> Colossians 2:8

I was recently at the checkout counter at Kohl's department store and the tellers called for the manager to come and examine what she thought were counterfeit twenty-dollar bills. I watched as the manager held the bills up to the light as he looked for some specific evidence that the money was either genuine or fake. After the manager had dealt with the situation, I asked him if he had to check for counterfeit money on a regular basis. To my amazement, his response was, "all too often."

In a similar way, followers of Jesus have to constantly be on guard concerning what is true and what is false. We are surrounded with conflicting worldviews and conflicting ideas that could draw us away from our loyalty to Christ. It is no surprise to me to find warnings in scripture to be on high alert against false teachers. As Paul writes to the church in Colosse: "See to it that no one takes you captive through hollow and deceptive philosophy, which depends on human tradition and the elemental spiritual forces of this world rather than on Christ" (Colossians 2:8).

In this verse Paul sees false teachers as a threat to those who have embraced the true gospel. He believes these false teachers are seeking to lead us into "spiritual captivity" by means of "wrongheaded religion". Although Paul uses the word philosophy, which means love of wisdom, he is referring to false religion that is made up of human ideas mixed with ideas inspired by demons. The worst thing about their teachings is that they do not depend on who Christ is, what he taught, or what he accomplished on the cross.

This leads me back to my opening story about the manager having to be on guard against counterfeit money. I have often heard people say that the best way to know what is genuine currency verses what is counterfeit is to be familiar with the truly genuine. When it comes to the truth, I think the same reasoning applies.

When the Apostle Paul wrote letters to the churches helping them to discern truth from error, he strongly encouraged them to be grounded in what they were taught (Col 2:6-7), and to understand fully who Jesus was and what he accomplished for them (Col 2:9-15). If they would follow his advice, they would more easily discern what is true and what is false.

Friends we will always have to face "wrongheaded" ideas, ideas that will seek to lead us away from our relationship with Jesus Christ and away from his wonderful teachings. Let us, therefore, be on guard against such ideas and more importantly let us be truly grounded in what is true so that false ideas will be easily detected and quickly disregarded.

In closing, let me share several things that I have found helpful in "grounding" myself in faith.

- Prayerfully read the Bible asking key questions like these found in Appendix II.
- Read and study your church's statement of beliefs.
- Read a book on theology like Wayne Grudem's *Christian Beliefs*, John Stott's *Basic Christianity*, N.T. Wright *Simply Christian* or C.S. Lewis' *Mere Christianity*.
- Read a good book on Christian apologetics like Timothy Keller's *The Reason For God* or Josh McDowell's *More Than A Carpenter*.

REFLECTION QUESTIONS:

1. Do you sense that you are in a battle for truth? (If so explain).

2. What causes you to lose your confidence in Christ?

3. What do you do to ground yourself in the faith?

"Jesus Christ has true excellency,
and so great an excellency,
that when you come to see him
you look no further,
but your mind rests there."

— Jonathan Edwards (1703-1758)

IN HIM

> "Remain in me, and I will remain in you.
> No branch can bear fruit by itself; it must remain in the vine.
> Neither can you bear fruit unless you remain in me."
>
> John 15:4

One of the most exciting days in the life of an avid hockey fan is the NHL's draft day. For weeks preceding the draft, hard-core hockey fans will read newspaper articles and listen to hockey experts on radio or TV talk about possible draft picks who may become part of their favourite team. Of special interest to an avid fan is whom their team will pick in the first round. Although there is no guarantee that a first round pick will ever make the NHL, hockey fans love to believe that their team is getting a player that should have gone higher in the draft, and that one day their pick is going to be a very effective and productive player.

In many ways, followers of Jesus Christ share several things in common with a drafted hockey player. Firstly, like a drafted hockey player they are chosen, and secondly, they are chosen with the purpose of being productive. Both of these facts are clearly taught in John 15 where Jesus says: "You did not choose me, but I chose you and appointed you to go and bear fruit—fruit that will last" (John 15:16a). Jesus obviously chose us for a reason; he wants us to be productive—to bear fruit in our lives.

Earlier in John 15, Jesus teaches us the key to being a productive follower when he says, "Remain in me, and I will remain in you.

No branch can bear fruit by itself; it must remain in the vine. Neither can you bear fruit unless you remain in me" (John 15:4).

In John 15:1-10 we read the word "remain" repeated 11 times. The idea behind this word may best be captured in the phrase "staying vitally connected" to something or someone. Just as a branch can only produce fruit if it stays vitally connected to the vine, followers of Jesus can only produce fruit by staying vitally connected to him. In the words of Merrill Tenney: "The effectiveness of the believer depends on his receiving the constant flow of life from Christ."

Friends, we have been chosen by Christ for the purpose of being productive followers. He wants us to be fruitful, marked by love and good deeds. According to Jesus, a fruitful life comes only out of a relationship with him. As we stay close to Jesus—vitally connected to him—a productive, fruit-bearing life is inevitable. Let's do everything we can to remain in him!

REFLECTION QUESTIONS:

1. How does it make you feel to know that you have been chosen by Jesus Christ?
2. What prevents you from staying close to Jesus?
3. What activities help you stay close to Jesus?

"By the very definition of following,
 we are called to a deepening intimacy with Christ…
 For followers, Christianity is a relationship,
 or adventure; a passionate pursuit of Christ."[15]

— Joseph Stowell

---

15 Joseph Stowell, *Following Christ* (Chicago, Illinois: Moody Press, 1998).

HIM

> "Never be lacking in zeal, but keep your spiritual fervour, serving the Lord."
>
> Romans 12:11

On several occasions, the congregation at Summit Drive Church has heard Pastor Dave Mohr speak highly of his father. When Dave spoke on Colossians 3:23-24, he once again spoke of his father in affectionate terms. Recently that caused me to ask Dave if Colossians 3:23-24 was, in fact, his father's favourite passage? In reply, Dave said that he wasn't sure if that was his father's favourite verse but one thing for sure, he lived it.

Dave went on to tell me that when his dad entered retirement, he spent hours doing volunteer work for his church. When he served as church chairman, he would often put in 15-20 hours a week caring for the church. Furthermore, when his father spoke about the church, he would often quote that passage in Colossians, as if to say this is how all Christians should function.

Dave's first encounter with this great passage, however, was not all that pleasant. As a young man, he would on occasion hear his dad quote this passage if he was doing his farm chores in a less-than enthusiastic manner. In those moments, the words of the Apostle Paul would pour forth from his fathers' mouth: "Whatever you do, work at it with all your heart, as working for the Lord, not for men, since you know that you will receive an inheritance from the

Lord as a reward. It is the Lord you are serving" (Col 3:23-24). Although Dave's first experience with these words of scripture came as correction, they have become precious to him as he seeks to serve the Lord and encourage others to do the same.

Serving the Lord is what followers of Jesus Christ do as a way of life. Christ calls his followers to a life of humble service and clearly wants them to use their time, talents and gifts to build up his church and to bless others as they take a service mentality into all they do.

Can you imagine what any given church would look like if everyone attending served in some way? Obviously it would be an incredible church where people would be ministered to in many wonderful ways, and most definitely, a church where all its ministries would be fully staffed. For this reason we make it a yearly goal at Summit that at least 80% of those attending our church should be included in some form of service in or outside our church. It's also why all the staff members at Summit seek to have a volunteer dimension to their ministry.

Friends, we live in a busy world where people are often encouraged, expected or tempted to work far too many hours per week. As well, we live in a world where recreational activities are always before us. It's into this world that we are called to serve the Lord. Although it is quite natural for followers to lose their passion for service, Jesus certainly calls us to a life of passionate service. As his servant the Apostle Paul writes: "Never be lacking in zeal, but keep your spiritual fervour, serving the Lord" (Romans 12:11). In just 13 words Paul says a great deal about what Christian service is all about. Firstly, it's about serving with great passion as we give our best for Him. Secondly, it's about being strengthened by the Holy Spirit for service. And thirdly, it's about doing everything we do as if we were doing it for the Lord himself. Let's serve well, for serving the Lord is most certainly an appropriate response to Jesus.

REFLECTION QUESTIONS:

1. What is one of your most memorable service projects or volunteer roles?

2. How can serving as if we were doing it for Jesus himself, transform ordinary tasks?

3. What best motivates you to a life of service?

"This is the true joy of life: the being used up
for a purpose recognized by yourself as a mighty one;
being a force of nature, instead of a feverish,
selfish little clot of ailments and grievances,
complaining that the world
will not devote itself
to making you happy."

— George Bernard Shaw

Trust
HIM

> "Do not let your hearts be troubled.
> Trust in God, "trust also in me".
>
> John 14:1

When travelling to eight different countries in just twelve days, my wife Lori and I had to adjust quickly to the different currencies being used. Can it ever be confusing! Often you will find yourself looking at a handful of strange currency wondering what you should give to the teller at the shop or restaurant. On more than one occasion, I simply held out a handful of money and let the teller take what was needed. Although the teller could have taken more money than necessary, I chose to trust them to do the right thing.

In an even greater way, Jesus calls us to trust him. In John's gospel, Jesus says: "Do not let your hearts be troubled. Trust in God; trust also in me" (John 14:1). Let me explain the context into which Jesus spoke these challenging words.

Following a Passover meal with his twelve disciples, Jesus sadly predicted that one of his disciples would betray him. The disciples were baffled at who that might be, except for Judas who left to find the Jewish leaders and betray Jesus to them.

After Judas' departure, Jesus told his disciples that he was going to leave them and that they could not come with him at this time. In response, Peter wanted to know where Jesus was going. He was determined to follow him wherever he was going and wanted to know why he could not come now. Surprisingly, Jesus answered Peter by telling him that he was going to deny him three times before the rooster crowed the next morning.

Peter was, no doubt, bewildered by Christ's prediction of his impending disloyalty, as well as bewildered by Jesus' comments that he was leaving the disciples. It was into this perplexing and uncertain situation that Jesus called his disciples to trust in both God and in him.

Immediately following his command to trust him, Jesus then makes several promises that his disciples needed to both hear and affirm at the center of their beings. Firstly, Jesus says he was going away to prepare a place for them, and secondly, that he will come back for his disciples so that they can be with him forever. What incredible promises! Jesus is preparing a place for his disciples. Furthermore, he is going to come back so that he can take us to be with him forever.

Although Jesus' disciples were bewildered and confused concerning his impending departure, Jesus called them to trust him. Specifically, Jesus wanted them to trust him in his absence, and he wanted them to trust him regarding their eternal destiny. Today, Jesus is still calling his followers to trust him for our every need, and yes, our eternal destiny. Will we trust him?

REFLECTION QUESTIONS:

1. What areas of your life do you need to trust Jesus in?

2. What keeps you from trusting Jesus?

3. What makes trusting Jesus easier?

"God chose the radical tactic of self-sacrifice to reveal that he is the leader we can trust."[16]

— Jan David Hettinga

---

16 Jan David Hettinga, *Follow Me: Experiencing the Loving Leadership of Jesus* (Colorado Springs, Colorado: Navpress, 1996).

Understand
WHO
HE IS

> "But grow in the grace and knowledge
> of our Lord and Saviour Jesus Christ."
>
> 2 Peter 3:18a

On Sunday, July 24, 2011, Pastor Dave Fields spoke at Summit Drive Church on two familiar stories found in Mark's gospel. We all know the stories: The feeding of the five thousand and Jesus' walking on the water (Mark 6:30-52). Although these two miracles are well known to most Bible readers, I doubt most people understand why Jesus did these miracles in the first place. As Dave pointed out, Jesus did these miracles so that his disciples would come to understand his true identity and ultimately, trust his leadership.

Dave began his message by quoting A.W. Tozer: "What comes to your mind when we think about God is the most important thing about you." The reason Dave shared this quote is because when it comes to Jesus, we often do not take following him seriously enough because we do not have a proper understanding of who he really is. So, in Mark's gospel, Jesus performs two amazing miracles that teach us that he is actually God himself, present with us in the person of Jesus.

In the two stories we discover that Jesus does what only God can do. What God does in the Old Testament, Jesus does as well. God feeds the people of Israel in the wilderness (Exodus 16:1ff);

so does Jesus. God leads people to green pastures (Psalm 23); so does Jesus. The book of Job tells us that God walks on the waves of the water (Job 9:8), and then we see Jesus doing, really, what only God can do. God passes by his servants Moses and Elijah to reveal his identity to them (Exodus 34:6; 1 Kings 19:11). So too, Jesus "passes by" his disciples to reveal his true identity as the divine Son of God. The similarities between what God did in the Old Testament and what Jesus does in these two stories are too great to overlook. Readers of these stories should conclude that Jesus is God in flesh, and if so, he must be taken seriously.

It's no wonder that the Apostle Peter insists that we grow in our understanding of Jesus. We read in his second letter: "But grow in the grace and knowledge of our Lord Jesus Christ" (3:18). To grow in the grace of Jesus is to grow in the virtues that are ours in Christ (2 Peter 1:5-8). To grow in the knowledge of Jesus is also to have a growing and deeply personal relationship with Jesus; much like the knowledge very close friends have of each other.

I am convinced that as we grow in our knowledge and understanding of Jesus, we will not only be able to stand firm in our faith, but we will more readily respond to Jesus in appropriate ways. As we come to understand who he is in the depth of our being—that he is the wisest man who ever lived, that he is the Son of God, God in the flesh, and our Creator—we will be much more likely to respond to everything he is calling us to do. It's no wonder Peter calls us to grow in the knowledge of Jesus. To truly know him will lead us to fully trust him. May we all make it a goal of first importance to grow in the grace and knowledge of Jesus.

REFLECTION QUESTIONS:

1. What helps you to grow in the knowledge of Jesus?

2. How is honouring and obeying Jesus made easier when you really understand whom Jesus is?

3. In what sense do we begin to really understand ourselves through understanding who Jesus is (see quote below)?

"Not only do we not know God
except through Jesus Christ:
we do not even know ourselves
except through Jesus Christ."

— Blaise Pascal (1623-1662)

Vocalize Our Allegiance TO HIM

"Whoever acknowledges me before others,
I will also acknowledge before my Father in heaven."

Matthew 10:32

I went through a period in my life where I was being challenged to be more vocal about my commitment to Jesus Christ. When you are consciously thinking this way, it is amazing how many opportunities you are given to talk to others about your faith in Christ. Let me tell you about one of these opportunities.

I was standing in the Aberdeen Hills Pro Shop after playing nine holes on one of their men's nights. As I looked around the Pro Shop I noticed two men I had never seen before, so I introduced myself to them. After briefly talking about their golf experience, we began to talk about our jobs in our community. As the conversation progressed, I told them I was a Baptist minister who was looking forward to a summer sabbatical when I was going to attempt to write a short book.

In short order, one of the gentlemen asked me what my book was going to be about. I told them that I believe that we were created by Christ, and for Christ, and so I was going to write a book on how we should respond to him today. I was grateful for that opportunity to tell them of why I believe God created us—that we are valued and have purpose. To my delight they seemed interested in what I had to say.

Where did this desire come from to be more open about my faith in Christ? To be honest, it came as a result of studying the New Testament and searching out how we should respond to Jesus today. In Matthew's gospel we read these words of Jesus: "Whoever acknowledges me before others, I will also acknowledge before my Father in heaven" (Matthew 10:32). Although I have read this verse many, many times before, only recently has it challenged me to be more open about my faith. And what really excites me about this passage is that if we acknowledge Jesus before people, he will also acknowledge us before his Father in heaven. I want Jesus to acknowledge me before my Father in heaven. This truth is motivating me to be more open about my relationship with Jesus.

It is my conviction that we are all given opportunities to declare our allegiance to Jesus Christ. Let me share a few examples.

- At your baptism, you have an opportunity to declare your allegiance to Jesus (especially before the guests you invited).
- When asked why you will not engage in a certain activity, you could say: "My best friend Jesus wouldn't approve."
- When someone asks you why you do not swear, you could respond by simply saying: "I could never curse the person I love."
- When thanked by someone for something you have done, you could respond by saying: "You know, Jesus is always motivating me to do such things."

May I suggest that there will be countless opportunities for us to vocalize our allegiance to Jesus Christ? Let's seize every opportunity we are given and ask Jesus for more opportunities to acknowledge him before others.

REFLECTION QUESTIONS:

1. Can you think of a situation when you failed to confess your allegiance to Jesus Christ?

2. How do you feel when you succeed in acknowledging Jesus before others?

3. What would encourage you to be more open about your faith in Christ?

"I will declare my allegiance from the mountaintops, joining the chorus of the saints and martyrs. And I will raise the banner of love above all flags."[17]

— Shane Claiborne

---

[17] Shane Claiborne, *The Irresistible Revolution: Living as an Ordinary Radical* (Grand Rapids, Michigan: Zondervan, 2006) p. 194.

Worship HIM

"And again, when God brings his firstborn into the world, he says, 'Let all God's angels worship him.'"

Hebrews 1:6

In my understanding one of the greatest responses we could ever make to the person of Jesus Christ is that of worship—of yielding our lives to him and giving him praise and honour. That is exactly what the Father describes as the right response to Jesus in Hebrews: "And again, when God brings his firstborn into the world, he says, 'Let all God's angels worship Him'" (Hebrews 1:6).

We need to understand fully the significance of this verse. God himself is calling his angels to worship his Son, Jesus Christ. The writer of Hebrews is arguing that the Son is worthy of worship by the angels because he's much "greater" than they are. Jesus is not an angel: no, he is worthy of worship in the same way as God the Father. And as we see, not only is worship of Jesus the right response for the angels; it is for us to. In Matthew's gospel, after Jesus' resurrection, we see two specific examples of his first followers worshipping him: "They [Mary Magdalene and the other Mary] clasped his feet and worshipped him" (Matthew 28:9b); "When they [the eleven disciples] saw him, they worshipped him…" (Matt 28:17a). For both the angels, and for us, worship is the right response to Jesus.

If you were to take a few minutes to read Hebrews 1, you would be reminded why Jesus is worthy of worship. For example, in this great chapter of scripture, Jesus is...

- The one through whom God made the universe (v. 2)
- The radiance of God's glory (v. 3)
- The exact representation of God's being (v. 3)
- The one who holds all things together (v. 3)
- The one who provided purification from sin (v. 3)
- The one who sits at the Father's right hand (v. 3, 13)
- The one the Father calls "God" (v. 8)

For these reasons and more, it is appropriate to worship Jesus Christ. As theologian Millard Erickson writes: "Worship of Christ is appropriate. He is not merely the highest of creatures, but he is God in the same sense and to the same degree as the Father. He is deserving of our praise, adoration, and obedience as is the Father."[18]

It is no wonder that we read of the disciples worshipping Jesus (Matt 28:17). Furthermore, in the book of Revelation we read of Jesus being worshipped along with the Father, by every creature in heaven and earth (Rev 5:13-14). Of note in Revelation 5, Jesus is worshipped not only because his sacrificial death entitled him to open the scrolls, which revealed the unfolding mysteries of God's plan for the world, but also because he possesses the same qualities as God himself (compare Rev 5:12 and 7:12).

It is for these reasons—and more—that the church continues to worship God as Father, Son and Holy Spirit. I conclude, then, by saying that when it comes to responding to Jesus, you can do no better than when you truly worship him.

---

18 Millard Erickson, *Christian Theology – Volume 2* (Grand Rapids, Michigan: Baker Book House, 1985) p. 704

REFLECTION QUESTIONS:

1. According to Hebrews 1:6, who is calling the angels to worship Jesus the Son?

2. Why is the worship of Jesus Christ such an appropriate response to him?

3. What effect does the worship of God (Father, Son and Holy Spirit) have upon you?

"Praise God from whom all blessing flow.
Praise him all creatures here below.
Praise him, ye heavenly hosts.
Praise Father, Son and Holy Ghost."

— Thomas Ken

Xtra Love for Him

> "If anyone comes to me and does not hate father and mother, wife and children, brothers and sisters—yes, even their own life—such a person cannot be my disciple."
>
> Luke 14:26

In the popular DVD series *Parenting God's Way*, the Ezzos make a strong case that the primary relationship in any family should be that of the husband and wife. Although they go to great lengths to teach parents how to love their children, they firmly believe that the husband and wife relationship is truly primary in any home. To support their conviction, they point to the obvious fact that parents raise their children to leave home. Yes, eventually the parents will be left "all alone."

The Ezzos argue that children are indeed more secure when they know that mom and dad really love each other and they strongly believe that the primacy of the husband and wife relationship helps children realize that the world does not revolve around them. For these reasons and more, the Ezzos argue that the husband and wife's love for each other is even more important than their love for their children.

This is a concept I struggled with at first but from observation I must say that when I see one partner loving and honouring their children over their spouse, I sense something is really wrong. The Ezzos have convinced me that my love for my wife is even more important than the love I have for my children.

Jesus himself taught us to love in a discriminatory manner too, didn't he? In Luke's gospel we discover this challenging, difficult verse of scripture: "If anyone comes to me and does not hate father and mother, wife and children, brothers and sisters—yes, even their own life—such a person cannot be my disciple" (Luke 14:26). What is Jesus trying to teach us? In my understanding, Jesus is not teaching us to actually hate our loved ones because we know that he truly wants us to honour and love our parents (Mark 7:9-13), and to even love our enemies (Luke 5:27). Nor is he calling us to hate ourselves, because he clearly taught us to love our neighbours *as ourselves* (Matthew 22:29). So then, what *is* Jesus trying to teach us? I believe he is teaching us that our love for him and his kingdom should come first. We must truly love him more than family—even our own life.

I believe this is the correct understanding of this challenging verse for the following reasons. Although the word "hate" usually means hate, it can also mean, "to love less." Jesus often uses hyperbole—exaggeration to make a point—in his teaching. The fact that Jesus was using hyperbole in Luke's gospel is supported by a verse in Matthews' gospel: "Anyone who loves his father and mother more than me is not worthy of me; anyone who loves his son or daughter more than me is not worthy of me" (Matt 10:37).

As well, Christ's teaching that we must put him first is consistent with his response to the question, "which is the greatest commandment?" According to Jesus, the greatest commandment is love God with all our hearts (Matt 22:37), and the second greatest commandment is to love our neighbour as ourselves (Matt 22:39). When one considers the fact that in numerous passages Jesus is called God, loving him above others is indeed our appropriate response (see Appendix IV).

In this challenging passage of scripture, Jesus is calling us to love him more than any other person; including our loved ones. In the words of New Testament scholar F.F. Bruce: "The interest of God's kingdom must be paramount with the followers of

Jesus, and everything else must take second place to him, even family ties."[19]

As I reflected on this verse, it occurred to me that when I, in fact, love Jesus first, I do not love others less. I say that because when I love him first he causes me to love others in a more thoughtful and caring manner. So you might say that loving Jesus first is the key to all my relationships. Yes, when I put Jesus first, my family, friends and neighbours will be much more blessed as well.

REFLECTION QUESTIONS:

1. The meaning of "hate" in Luke 14:26 is best understood to mean, "love less". Do you agree or disagree and why?
2. Why can Jesus legitimately call on us to love him more than our family?
3. How can loving Jesus more than anyone else help us to love others in profound ways?

"No one who has authentically followed him [Jesus] without compromise has become disillusioned or found his ways to be disappointing."[20]

— Joseph Stowell

---

19 F.F. Bruce, *The Hard Sayings of Jesus* (Downers Grove, Illinois: InterVarsity Press) p. 119.
20 Stowell, *Following Christ*

Yield to His LEADING

"When they came to the border of Mysia, they tried to enter Bithynia, but the Spirit of Jesus would not allow them to."

Acts 16:7

During the winter of 2010-2011, I often found myself walking the indoor track at the Tournament Capital Center on the campus of Thompson Rivers University. On one occasion, I was all alone walking the track, which allowed me to pray. As I recall, it was a time of prayer where I sensed a wonderful closeness to God. After walking the track, I went to the exercise equipment near the track and began to use one machine after another. Within a few minutes, a staff member came by of whom I was prompted to ask several questions regarding his job at the Tournament Capital Center. He was a very engaging individual, and it wasn't long before we were in a lengthy discussion concerning the person of Jesus Christ.

As I reflected on that opportunity, it occurred to me that I was being led by the Spirit of God to share Christ with him. In many ways it felt like a "divine set up." Of note, several weeks later I discovered that another member of Summit Drive Church had also been witnessing to the very same person. In my opinion, the Spirit of Jesus was leading us both to share our faith with him.

In the New Testament we read of the Spirit of Jesus at work leading the Apostle Paul and his companions in their missionary efforts. For example, in Acts 16 we read:

> "Paul and his companions traveled throughout the region of Phrygia and Galatia, having been kept by the Holy Spirit from preaching the word in the province of Asia. ⁷When they came to the border of Mysia, they tried to enter Bithynia, but the Spirit of Jesus would not allow them to. ⁸So they passed by Mysia and went down to Troas. ⁹ During the night Paul had a vision of a man of Macedonia standing and begging him, "Come over to Macedonia and help us." ¹⁰ After Paul had seen the vision, we got ready at once to leave for Macedonia, concluding that God had called us to preach the gospel to them" (16:6-10).

In this passage we see God clearly leading Paul and his companions. In verse six the Holy Spirit kept them from preaching the word in the province of Asia. Likewise, the Spirit of Jesus would not allow them to enter Bithynia (v. 7). It was only after Paul had received a vision in the night inviting them to preach the gospel in Macedonia that they concluded God had called them there. Although the Apostle Paul was very much a strategic planner when it came to missions, he was also keenly aware of the role of the Holy Spirit. (Of note, in 16:6-10 we find these words "the Holy Spirit", and the "Spirit of Jesus" and "God" used interchangeably to describe who was giving Paul direction in his missionary efforts. Passages like these clearly support the Christian doctrine of the Trinity).

When we think of the Holy Spirit's role in our lives, we most quickly think of the Spirit's work in helping us to say "no" to sin and "yes" to virtue. We can go to the fifth chapter of Galatians, where Paul exhorts us to "live by the Spirit" and to "keep in step with the Spirit", but as we have seen in the book of Acts, the Spirit of Jesus also works to lead his people into missionary activity. Bible readers should conclude that, effective evangelism is a Spirit led activity.

In the month of December 2010, I believe the Spirit of Jesus led us to team up with the country band, High Valley, resulting in over 450 guests hearing the gospel at our annual Christmas outreach event. I believe this was a Spirit led event because we had prayed for just the right "entertainment" and amazingly, they phoned us inquiring if we could possibly host them for a concert (this was the first time they ever played at the same venue on three straight nights).

Such an experience has encouraged me to be sensitive to the leading of the Spirit as I seek to spread the good news.

REFLECTION QUESTIONS:

1. What is the first thing you think of when you hear the term Holy Spirit?

2. Can you think of a time you were definitely led by the Spirit to witness to someone?

3. How can we learn to be more sensitive to the leading of the "Spirit of Jesus"?

"The Spirit of Christ is the spirit of mission,
and the nearer we get to him,
the more intensely missionary we become."[21]

— Henry Martyn

---

21 Henry Martyn, as quoted in *The Christian Quote Book*. p. 14

Zoom in on HIM

> "Let us fix our eyes on Jesus, the author and perfecter of our faith, who for the joy set before him endured the cross, scorning its shame, and sat down at the right hand of the throne of God."
>
> Hebrews 12:2

Historians report that more Christians suffered persecution in the 20th century than in all the other centuries combined.[22] Even today, millions of Christians are being persecuted simply because they are followers of Jesus. Fortunately, followers of Christ living in North America today have not experienced the same type of persecution that many have suffered throughout our world.

Yet despite the wonderful freedom we enjoy, many North American Christians have become discouraged. They can be discouraged by the fact that they know people who have walked away from the faith. They can be discouraged by the growth of gangs and crime in their cities, by what they feel is a growing secularization of their nation, and even by their own failure to live out their faith in the way they think they should.

If you feel yourself discouraged for any of the above reasons, I encourage you with these timeless words: "Let us fix our eyes on Jesus, the author and perfecter of our faith, who for the joy set before him endured the cross, scorning its shame, and sat down at the right hand of the throne of God" (Hebrews 12:2).

---

[22] David B. Barrett and Todd M. Johnson "World Christian Trends AD 30- AD 2200: Interpreting the annual Christian Megacensus" (Pasadena, California: William Carey Library, 2001). p. 229. In this study the authors report that in 2000 years of Christian history, approximately 70 million Christians have been killed because of their faith. Of that number, 45 million were killed in the 20th century alone.

This passage was originally written to a group of believers who were facing severe persecution and hardships because of their faith (10:32-34). The persecution was so severe that some were tempted to stop following Jesus altogether (10:35-39). In the face of such opposition, the author of Hebrews challenged them to stay focused on Jesus; to stay focused on the one who gave them faith in the first place; to stay focused on the one who will perfect their faith; to stay focused on the one who gave his life for them; and yes, to stay focused on the one who now triumphantly sits at God's right hand. In staying focused on Jesus they would find the motivation to overcome the temptation to turn away from the faith.

In the previous verse (12:1), the writer encouraged them to consider the fact that other followers had been faithful, even in the midst of their challenges. As well, he encouraged them to rid themselves of anything, including any specific sin that would keep them from faithfully following Jesus.

The idea of staying focused on Jesus seems to be the author's most important advice to those facing persecution. I say that because in the very next verse he writes: "Consider him who endured such opposition from sinful men, so that you will not grow weary and lose heart" (12:3). In this verse, the writer is once again asking his readers to consider thoughtfully what Christ has done for them on the cross so that they would not lose heart in the face of persecution. It should also be noted that in chapter 3, the author had encouraged the recipients with a similar exhortation: "Therefore, holy brothers and sisters, who share in the heavenly calling, fix your thoughts on Jesus, the apostle and high priest whom we confess" (Hebrews 3:1).

According to the writer of Hebrews, staying focused on Jesus in the face of persecution seems to be the key to overcoming the temptation to shrink back from the faith. May I suggest that staying focused on Jesus is also the key to living a life of faith when you find yourself discouraged? As we seek to remain faithful to our great calling, let's make sure we stay focused on Jesus.

REFLECTION QUESTIONS:

1. What are some "good things" that can keep you from following Jesus?

2. How does Christ's example of endurance and suffering motivate you to stay faithful?

3. In practical terms, how can we fix our eyes on Jesus?

"Tell me what you pay attention to
and I will tell you who you are."

— Jose Ortega y Gasset

AUTHOR'S CHALLENGE

I believe following Jesus involves both the grace of God at work in us (Phil 2:13) and, at least in part, something we need to actively do as well (Phil 2:12). Although God is powerfully at work in our lives (see Appendix I), we are nevertheless to respond to Jesus in some very specific ways. The purpose of this book was to give followers of Jesus an overview of the specific ways in which we are to respond to him today. So in closing, let me challenge you to memorize all 26 appropriate and biblical responses to Jesus.

In addition, let me encourage you to memorize the corresponding verses of scriptures found in the alphabetical tool. As I said earlier, if you memorize all of the appropriate responses to Jesus, and the corresponding verses, you can review them in your heart and mind wherever you are. To do so will truly help you to stay close to Jesus and be a caring, passionate follower of Jesus.

Your friend in Christ,
Harry Bicknell

APPENDIX 1

Keeping Our Part in Perspective

Spiritual growth takes thoughtful effort. If you want to become more like Jesus you will have to respond to him in the very specific ways found in the New Testament. Yes, you have a part to play in your spiritual development! Having said that, it must be clearly understood that discipleship and spiritual growth are not just about human effort, for when people come to faith, God works in their lives. Consider with me the following verses of Scripture:

Romans 8:29-30: *"For those God foreknew he also predestined to be conformed to the likeness of his Son, that he might be the firstborn among many brothers. ³⁰ And those he predestined, he also called; those he called, he also justified; those he justified, he also glorified."*

Romans 15:5: *"May the God who gives endurance and encouragement give you a spirit of unity among yourselves as you follow Christ Jesus..."*

Galatians 5:22-23: *"But the fruit of the Spirit is love, joy, peace, patience, kindness, goodness, faithfulness, gentleness and self-control."*

Philippians 1:6: *"Being confident of this, that he who began a good work in you will carry it on to completion until the day of Christ Jesus."*

Philippians 2:13: *"...for it is God who works in you to will and to act according to his good purpose."*

1 Corinthians 1:8-9: *"He will keep you strong to the end, so that you will be blameless on the day of our Lord Jesus Christ. ⁹ God, who has called you into fellowship with his Son Jesus Christ our Lord, is faithful."*

2 Corinthians 1:21-22: *"Now it is God who makes both us and you stand firm in Christ, he anointed us, set his seal of ownership on us, and put his Spirit in our hearts as a deposit, guaranteeing what is to come."*

1 Thessalonians 5:23-24: *"May God himself, the God of peace, sanctify you through and through. May your whole spirit, soul and body be kept blameless at the coming of our Lord Jesus Christ. The one who calls you is faithful and he will do it."*

Titus 2:11-13: *"For the grace of God that brings salvation has appeared to all people. It teaches us to say "No" to ungodliness and worldly passions, and to live self-controlled, upright and godly lives in this present age, while we wait for the blessed hope—the glorious appearing of our great God and Saviour, Jesus Christ…"*

In all our efforts to respond appropriately to Jesus, let us never forget that God is at work in our lives, empowering us to grow!

APPENDIX 11

How to Feed Yourself Spiritually

I believe all followers of Jesus can set aside at least 10 minutes a day to read and reflect on the Bible. If you do not already have a plan to read and reflect on scripture, let me suggest that you consider the following plan: follow a "read through the New Testament in a year" reading plan or simply purchase a "One Year Bible", where the entire Bible is divided into 365 readings.

Did you know that it would take you less than five minutes a day to read through the New Testament in a year? If, in addition to prayerfully reading a passage in the New Testament each day, you took another five minutes to reflect on what you read, you would be strengthened spiritually.

Here are some simple yet profound questions you could ask of each passage you read that would help you to both understand and apply the word of God to your life.

What does this passage teach me about...

- God the Father?
- Jesus Christ?
- The Holy Spirit?
- Humanity?

Are there any (SPECS)...

- Sins to confess?
- Promises to claim?
- Examples to follow?
- Commands to obey?
- Statements of significance?

One could, of course, spend more than ten minutes a day reading, reflecting and praying through scripture. Many people do, but

I offer this plan as a good starting place. One thing for sure, followers of Jesus Christ need to have a plan to feed themselves!

"Other books were given to us for information,
 but the Bible was given to us for transformation."
— Unknown

APPENDIX III

Summit Drive Mission Statement

We exist to glorify God by developing caring, passionate followers of Jesus Christ committed to loving relationships, ministry, spiritual growth, evangelism and worship.

APPENDIX IV

The Deity of Jesus Christ

The study of Scripture has led Christians to believe in the doctrine of the Trinity, which states that God is one being who exists eternally in three persons: Father, Son and Holy Spirit. In this document I will share why Christians believe that Jesus Christ is God along with the Father and the Spirit.

1. **Jesus is called God**
   - By John the apostle *(John 1:1; 1 John 5:20)*
   - By Thomas the apostle *(John 20:28)*
   - By Paul the apostle *(Romans 9:5; Titus 2:13)*
   - By the writer of Hebrews *(Hebrews 1:8)*
     (Here the Father addresses Jesus as "God" using a quote from Psalm 45:6-7)
   - By Isaiah the prophet
     (Isaiah 9:6; compare Isaiah 9:6 with Isaiah 10:21)

2. **In the Greek New Testament Lord (Greek: kyrios) is used to identify both God and Jesus**
   - Compare Matthew 11:25 and Acts 17:24 with John 20:28, Acts 10:36 and Philippians 2:11
   - In some passages Lord could refer to either Father or Son *(Acts 1:24, 2:47, 8:39, 9:31, 16:14)*

3. **Old Testament quotations referring to God are applied to Jesus**
   - Compare Acts 2:21 and Romans 10:13 with Joel 2:32
   - Compare Philippians 2:9-11 with Isaiah 45:23-24

4. **Jesus was given the name Immanuel which means God with us** *(Matthew 1:23 and see also Isaiah 7:14)*

5. **Jesus uses the divine Old Testament title "I Am" of himself** *(John 8:24, 28, 58)*
   - "I Am" denotes existence
     (Compare with Exodus 3:14-15)
   - Paul says Jesus is "before all things"
     (Colossians 1:17 and also John 1:1)

6. **To see Jesus is to see God**
   - Jesus "is the radiance of God's glory and the exact representation of his being" *(Hebrews 1:3)*
   - "The image of the invisible God" *(Colossians 1:15)*
   - "In Christ all the fullness of Deity lives in bodily form" *(Colossians 2:9, also 1:19)*.

7. **Jesus claimed to be one with the Father** *(John 10:3)*; **that to see him was to see the Father** *(John 14:7-9)*

8. **Jesus and the Father are both called…**
   - Saviour *(Compare Titus 1:3-4, 2:10, 3:4 with Titus 2:13, 3:6)*
   - King *(Compare 2 Timothy 6:15; Psalm 145:1 with Revelation 17:14, 19:16)*
   - "The first and last"
     (Compare Revelation 1:17 with Isaiah 41:4, 44:6, 48:12)
   - "The Alpha and Omega"
     (Revelation 22:13 with Revelation 1:8)

9. **Jesus claimed he should be honoured just like the Father is honoured** *(John 5:21)*

10. **Jesus claimed to be the Son of God** *(Mark 14:61-62)* **and in response the Jewish leaders condemned him to be worthy of death** *(Mark 14:63-65)*

11. **The Jews understood Jesus to be ...**
    - Making himself equal to God *(John 5:18)*
    - Claiming to be God *(John 10:33)*—
      and Jesus never denies their understanding

12. **Jesus and God are both worshipped by every creature under heaven** *(Revelation 5:13-14, 22:8-9)*
    - Of note, Jesus said only God is to be worshipped (Matthew 4:10) and it is clear that he allowed his followers to worship him *(Matthew 14:33, 28:9,17)*
    - Unlike the angel in Revelation 22:8-9, who forbids people from worshipping anyone but God, Jesus receives worship.

13. **Jesus does what God alone does**
    - Creates the world
      (Genesis 1:1; Colossians 1:16; Hebrews 1:2)
    - Promises his eternal presence
      (Compare Exodus 33:14-17 with Matthew 28:20)
    - Holds the world together *(Colossians 1:17)*
    - Gives life *(John 5:21)*
    - Forgives sin against God *(Mark 2:5,7)*
    - Judge of all humanity *(Compare Matthew 25:31-46 and 2 Timothy 4:1 with Hebrews 13:23)*
    - Gives grace *(2 Corinthians 13:14)*
      and comfort *(2 Thessalonians 2:16-17)*

14. Jesus claims…
    - To be omnipresent (Matthew 18:20, 28:20)
    - That the angels are his
      (Compare Matthew 13:41 with Luke 12:8-9)
    - The kingdom of God/Heaven is his
      (Compare Matthew 13:41 with Luke 6:20)
    - To have authority over the Sabbath
      (Compare Mark 2:27-28 with Exodus 20:8-11)
    - To have authority of the law *(Matthew 5-7)*
    - To have authority over both heaven and earth
      (Matthew 28:18)

15. **The church is instructed to baptize new followers in the name (singular) of the Father, Son and Holy Spirit** *(Matthew 28:19)*

16. **Jesus is in nature God and is equal to God**
    (Philippians 2:6)
    - One day everyone will recognise this
      (Philippians 2:9-11)

APPENDIX V

Recommended Readings on Christian Living and Discipleship

Finding the Will of God *by Bruce Waltke*

Following Christ *by Joseph Stowell*

Following Jesus: Biblical Reflections on Discipleship *by NT Wright*

Follow Me *by Jan Hettinga*

How Good is Good Enough? *by Andy Stanley*

My Heart Christ's Home *by Robert Munger*

Purpose Driven Life *by Rick Warren*

The Reason for God *by Timothy Keller*

The Life God Rewards *by Bruce Wilkinson*

The Practise of Godliness *by Jerry Bridges*

The Disciplines of Grace *by Jerry Bridges*

What's So Amazing about Grace *by Philip Yancey*

APPENDIX VI

Additional Biblical responses to Jesus that are not listed in the alphabetical tool

1. Call on his name *(Romans 10:13, 1 Corinthians 1:2)*
2. Clothe yourself with him *(Romans 13:14)*
3. Confess him as Lord *(Romans 10:9)*
4. Come to him *(1 Peter 2:4)*
5. Have faith in him *(Galatians 2:20b)*
6. Live for him *(2 Corinthians 5:15)*
7. Listen to him *(Matthew 17:5)*
8. Love him *(Ephesians 6:24)*
9. Receive him *(John 1:12)*
10. Set him apart as Lord *(1 Peter 3:15a)*
11. Take every thought captive to him *(2 Corinthians 10:5)*
12. Take his yoke upon you *(Matthew 11:29)*
13. Rejoice in him *(Philippians 3:1)*

Manufactured by Amazon.ca
Bolton, ON